# SEEDS

**S**erendipitous
**E**nergy
**E**volving
**D**istinctly
**S**pontaneous

---

## WITHIN WORDS

LYN ABBOTT WESTBROOK

# The Author

Lyn
Honest, edgy, searching reader,
Daughter of Thelma and Lloyd
Sister of Butch and Ron
Wife of Tim
Mother of Luke, Amy and Tracey
Grandmother of Hadley, Kenley, Evan, Austin,
Trenton, Abby, Tori, Emily and Gauge
Great-Grandmother of Collin
Lover of family, friends, animals, books, good wine, and pictures
Feels in a hurry, curious, angry and thankful
Gives time, money, opinions and love
Fears failure, sickness and stupidity
Would like to write something to change the world
Resident of Washington, West By God Virginia
Westbrook

# Dedicated

To Tim who always thinks I can,

To Luke who always doubts what I know,

To Hadley who adds the melody to my lyric,

To Kenley who brings the joy to my days,

To Evan who gives me hope in the future

To Sharon who told me years ago to DO SOMETHING

To Carolyn who helped me overcome my fear

To all my family and friends who love me –

No matter what.


You ALL are the big rocks in my life.

# Table of Contents

# Old Age

**IS JUST ANOTHER WORD FOR FREEDOM**
To finally allow a good wallow inside
Give up pretense, let go of pride
To finally sink in to the joy or the sadness
And best of all yet – give into the madness

Not anger, upset or irrational rage
But allowed to be downright crazy with age
To cry when I feel and laugh till I'm sore
And talk to myself out loud in the store

To eat cereal in bed and steaks in the AM
Start collecting collections, and creating mayhem
Take astrology classes, and not read the classics
But search through the comics to answer my questions

To walk round in public and not give a damn
And proudly display: "This is who I am!"
No longer to hide behind powder and paint
At last to be rid of that she that I ain't!

To finally wear clothes that feel good on my skin
And not care about if they make me look thin
Then laughing out loud at the words drifting by
As some people say: "…the grace of God there go I."

# Sleep

Sleep slips silently away
Leaving me in restless wakefulness
What seemed a sure thing moments ago
Now escapes with the whisper of angels
I feel the gossamer stroke of their wings
Brush my cheek as they escape to lands beyond my grasp
With my sleep solidly in their small silver hands

Locust post standing
At the edge of the graveyard
Spirits are silent

# The Road

The old road rambled
Forgotten among the Creek Willows
Past the Box Elders
And ended at the old shack
Ran right up to the porchless door
Hanging by one rusted hinge
And stopped – dead in its tracks
Waiting for some forgotten soul
To step out and remember
The way back

The mist turns to rain
Clouds appear in the distance
The feel of wet grass

# Vacation Vexation

If you're used to spending some time on your own
When driving to work and then driving home
If you go to bed early to read some at night
So you control blankets and the reading light

If you're used to having some space and some time
Where you can fuss, fidget, and write silly rhyme
Then being one of two people trapped in a car
Can become quite uncomfortable if you go very far

Then add to that tenseness the stupidity
Of all other drivers and you'll clearly see
How the most carefully planned and yearned for vacation
Can easily turn into a week-long vexation

The traffics too thick and my sweaters too thin
Cause the a/c's too cold in this car that I'm in
My normally sweet husband looks over at me
I'm sure the goose eggs on my arms he can see

Are you really too cold? He asks with a frown
It's so hot in here and turns the a/c further down
There's no one but idiots on this road that he sees
I look out my window and silently agree

Turn offs are missed and wrong turns are taken
The sports car he rented has my poor old back achin
Ten hours later, we arrive at our spot
Who packed all these over-stuffed bags that we've got?

How many shirts did I think I would wear?
But never once thought I might comb my hair
So everything's tossed into closets and drawers
And before we can rest we must dash to a store

Aspirins, deodorant, hair brush and comb
All of the things we left safely at home
Finally at last on the wee tiny deck
We watch ocean waves as the sun starts to set

Oh at last, here we are on a much needed vacation
Not a thing in the world could cause us vexation
Then the baby next door begins a shrill cry
And the drunks at the pool break into a fight

So we hurry inside to our cramped hotel room
I'm ever so tired, I'm sure I'll sleep soon
I'm always early to bed and here it's past ten
But my husband picks up the remote and just then

As he begins to flip channels I realize
He's never early to bed; he's up half the night!
I try not to panic, not to yell, not to weep
If I squeeze my eyes tight I'm sure I will sleep
But it's of no use, not with that old TV blaring
And soon I find myself mindlessly staring
At a stucco hotel room wall painted yellow
And I grow ever homesick for my room in the hollow

Oh what a week this is going to be
I say to myself as I watch the TV
Throw shadows across the old yellow wall
Then finally at last, into sleep I do fall

Now despite all my fears that I had that first night
The vacation itself turned out to be bright
We sight-saw and sunbathed and toured a bit
We ate and we laughed till our sides could have split

And although it's hard to have a summer vacation
Without there being some sort of summer vexation
It's well worth the trouble, the work and expense
And sometimes it's best when remembered past tense

# Ocean Waves

Mystery and Magic
Ride the foamy tide
To the moonlit beach
And crash to the sand
At my wandering feet

<br>

The mist turns to rain
Clouds appear in the distance
The feel of wet grass

# My Voice

My voice feels old
Like an old mountain woman
Down from the hills
To buy salt and flour
She needs nothing else

Most of the time
My voice is lost in the wind
And that's good enough
I rarely need to hear it
To know it's there

The tree fleeced in green
Cares not if clothed or naked
Simply thrilled to be

# The Plight of the Book Lover

Why did I spend fifty bucks at the book store
To buy more books when I already have more
Books than I have shelves to keep them?
My house is already a book land mayhem

My books are piled in every nook and corner
I constantly send in Amazon orders
Then cheerfully bestow another fifty on Borders
It's possible I could be a book hoarder.

I spend more money to buy more books
Instead of on clothes or how my hair looks
When I know that I can't possibly
Read more than two, well maybe three
Of those books at one time
And even at that I'm five years behind.

I walk across the frigid lot
Thinking of all the books I just bought
With the icy chill of winter air seeping
Into my collar, then slowly creeping
Down my spine, and tossing my hair
Despite all of it, I do not care
Cause my hearts full of joy, because there are
Fifty bucks worth of books waiting in my car.

I enter Wal-Mart and come face to face
With items I need like milk and hairspray
But instead of leaving with just those in my cart
I sneak in the only book I ain't got
The Anne Siddons novel that I haven't read
Slips into my buggy, right under the bread
Behind the milk, snuggled next to the hairspray
While my heart tells my head, "it's ok; it's ok."

I head for the checkout with credit card ready
I feel somewhat flushed, a little bit heady
Indulging myself, I know it's not right
Addiction to books is a terrible plight
There's no addicts meeting that I can be part of
To stop me from buying all these books that I love
But my face holds no guilt, just a big, silly grin
Lord there's no hope for the mess that I'm in.

Now right at this moment I cannot recall
The books I just bought while at the mall
But I'm sure of the truth and this truth is a fact
I need all those books, and that's simply that
They'll engage all my thoughts; they'll till my minds soil
They'll be my best friends, always there, always loyal

So despite all the money I've spent on my books
And regardless of all the piteous looks.
I've received from those people who don't understand
My addiction to books that I can't get in hand
I'll continue to buy them, each chance that I get
Cause I've never disliked a single one yet.

But I can't say the same for some people I've met.

# Making it Rhyme

I clean off my chair
And sit down at my desk
If it's rhyming they want
Then it's rhyming they'll get

I lay out my paper
Inspect it for dust
Pick up my blue pen
Check the nib end for rust

I doodle my name
I twirl my hair
I scratch at a bug bite
I spin round in my chair

I stare at the paper
It stares back at me
Despite all my plans
It's as blank as can be

Two hours later
My papers still bare
Except for some doodles
And small bits of hair

Finally at last
I accept who I am
I'm not good at rhyming
No, not worth a damn

I take out my notebook
And search through the pages
Surely I've written
Some rhyme through the ages

But alas, there is nothing
Not a rhyme on the place
I have nothing to offer
Oh what a disgrace!

# Seashore

The sound of the sea as it spills itself
Onto the soft sands of the shore at my feet
Fills my soul with its sentient spirit
Instilling a cool, serene swathe of stillness
Across the hot sands of my thoughts
Sinking me in a secluded peace

Dawns light
Falls goldenly
Chasing shadows away
The soul's moment of the day is
Daybreak

The beach
Made of soft sand
Created by the waves
Where soul and spirit meet as one
Seashore

# The World

There is edginess in this world,
A tightly wound spring
Waiting for the hair
To brush the trigger

There is desperate longing in this world,
Unspoken by human voice
Howled by the spirit
Wrenching the soul to attention

There is deep expectation in this world,
For something yet unknown
Something not yet proven
But desperately longed for

There is hideousness in this world,
Clothed in lies to make it bearable
Sharp and hunkered in a dark corner
Waiting to spring up stark and naked with truth

Still, there is calmness in this world,
A quiet knowing of all things necessary
A willingness to accept the unacceptable
A sacred knowledge that waits
In peaceful repose – for us.

# Crying Light

It is that early morning light
        Drifting across an inky black landscape
            More ethereal than visual

When my eyes perceive
        The arrival of a misty gray haze
            And that haze reaches into my heart

Like a darkroom chemical
        My heart envelops and develops the landscape
            It enters my eyes and falls into my soul

That moment when nothing
        Becomes something and then everything
            The angles and edges begin to take shape

That moment when I realize
        I am not a witness
            But that I Am

And tears wrung from gratitude
        For that enduring fact spill out
            My slowly brightening world blurs

That is the crying light
        That light that sparks an emotion
            That doesn't come often
                But that comes often enough
                    To not ever be forgotten

# The Magic Moment

Just as dusk fell
Magic flew through the air
Swaying tree tops and scattering leaves
In mini cyclones across the earth
And you knew
Something far beyond your understanding
Rules the universe

# Nothing To Lose

Alone in the dark with nowhere to turn
At the end of a rope – a lesson to learn
So many times I've been in this spot
Yet I paid no attention – the lesson untaught
I'd climb back up the rope, turn the lights on once more
And find myself back where I started before

If only I had the courage back then
To let go of the rope in the dark and fall in
I wouldn't be here in this place that I've made
Of repeated mistakes, and dreams tattered and frayed
The problem I have is each time I return
Back from the end with a lesson unlearned
I build this place stronger, the walls thick with age
What started as safety, has turned into a cage

So many of us sit in these places we've built
Foundations of fear, mortared with sorrow and guilt
Each day adding more random reasons to hide
From this glorious gift from God we call life
Instead, we should face the wisest of truths
New beginnings take place where there's **nothing to lose.**

# Fire

Orange, red and glowing amber
Ignites the heart and warms the feet
Gyrating wildly or quiet ember
Dancing to your sacred beat

Just a touch and you sustain us
A touch too much and you destroy
Yet we crave to gather round you
And express our love and joy

A tiny spark turns to inferno
Our hearts respond with awe and fear
Your spirit's essence blaze within you
You hold all the power here

From a scorched and blackened scarring
New life emerges, green again
You were there in the beginning
You will be here in the end

# Mornings

That first hour of another day
Those sixty minutes, more precious than gold
Yet many mornings in bed I lay
My body's too tired, my mind feels too old

But minutes wait for no man's pleasure
And missing life holds no reward
Finally at last I rouse to measure
The time that's lost, those minutes mourned

Now here I sit, the hour gone
The hands of time have swept it by
My heart, my soul, my spirit long
To wind them back and once more try

To live them as they should be lived
In consciousness and awe
Yet no mercy will time give
Moments gone and past are law

Written, carved in the stone of life
No chance to rewrite it ever
Those precious moments shining bright
Now are lost and gone forever

Each day I promise that on the morrow
I will jump up with gusto and be glad
Yet a part of me knows with simple sorrow
Instead I'll sleep, and then be sad.

# Traveling Limericks

I really do hate to fly in a plane
I hate it in sunshine at night or in rain
But it's too far to drive
So I just close my eyes
And hope when I get there I'm sane

I once few across the Atlantic
The flight made me simply quite frantic
Then when I arrived
And I saw how they drive
I traveled all week in a panic

# Wind

You coax leaves off their branches to float on the ground
Gently pushing and nudging and swirling round
Or jerking them wildly from their perch up above
And forcing them down with a strong blowing shove

From branches that held them for all of two seasons
Now you shower them round without any reasons
Tossing all in your path, in all four directions
As if it's all wrong and you're making corrections

With loud keeling, screaming, and wild banshee yells
You're crying of things our souls fear to tell
Our teeth set on edge by your unrestrained force
Till you've had your full say and run your full course

Then you gentle our nerves with your soft summer sighs
Telling stories of life our hearts recognize
Softly murmuring secrets through the tops of the trees
The language of love known by birds and by bees

With a last ragged breath you blast the old away
Then quietly whisper in a brand new day
You are powerful energy or gentle caress
And everything between, no more or no less

Without you we're nothing, we cease to exist
But consciously with you, we edge close to bliss
For blessed are those who honor your presence
For all ancient truth is held in your essence

Inside your cloak of invisibility
You hide ancient gifts of wisdom and creativity
Sometimes in a whirl of unrestrained charity
You scatter your gifts to all of humanity

Those who are careful to see where they lay
Can gather them up to carry away
But most of us stumble along in the blind
And miss what you offer, and leave it behind

# The Me Inside

I wish I could I wish I might
Be free of me that lives inside
She overtakes my thoughts and cares
She says those things I would not dare

Then after she's created havoc
She rides off like a western maverick
She leaves me standing in the dust
To deal with all the mess she's caused

I stand and look around in fright
And try to put her wrongs to right
But some things are beyond repair
And there's no way to mend the tear

I like me when I am alone
It's others who awake my clone
They drag her out into my day
She wrecks my world along her way

Small and large disasters trail
Behind her in my life's long tale
I am myself afraid to meet
Her face to face or cheek to cheek
She's stronger than I'll ever be
And she might see no need of me

She might cast me in the flame
And never have to take the blame

For all the trouble she has brought
Or all the hell that I have caught
I watch her from a safe, dark place
And hope to someday win the race

To be the first to speak out loud
With language that will make me proud
That speaks of love and truth of spirit
I pray to speak so all can hear it

So maybe on some far off day
I'll shut her up, I'll make her say
She's sorry for the things she's said
I hope it happens before I'm dead

# The Passing of a Summer Evening

I stand in the deep liquid darkness of an hour past sunset
And inhale the sweet, cool air of a newly born night
I hold it captive in my lungs, hold it, hold it…
I want to embrace the air, detain the moment
Keep the experience, and not let it pass

But just as life cannot hold more than this one moment
Lungs cannot hold more than this one breath
What is will not linger, and is now forever gone
The moment and my ethereal breath pass
Through my life, and are gone
Replaced by another and another…

While the moon lifts slowly, hauntingly beautiful
A luminescent orb rising over the eastern horizon
I release another breath into the liquid darkness
And a shooting star falls to earth
And is forever gone

# Exercising Time

I always plan to exercise
Each day of every week
Yet these plans turn into lies
Or plans that I forget to keep

I wake up early every morning
Plans in place, the coffee hot
The clock beside me ticks its warning
Drinking coffee – exercise it's not

Yet here I sit with coffee steaming
Books, papers, pens strewn round
Deep into this book I'm reading
No time to exercise is found

Oh no! The clock ticked past the warning
And no attention have I paid
The minutes are gone again this morning
Those plans the mice and I have laid

Have been swept up with minutes passing
Time for me to start my day
Inside, again my soul is laughing
I'd rather read, she seems to say

# Poetry to Me

Words thick on the page
Like home-churned yellow butter
That's been extra salted
With sweat and tears of a life
Still in process
Slathered across thin slabs
Of toasted parchment
In each bite – a lifetime
Flavored with the attempt
To immobilize the one bead of sweat
Or the one lone tear that
Represents existence

The words touch my ears
Their meaning misunderstood
Time silently stops

# Grandpa's Shoes

Tiny feet, translucent with youth
Tender in their innocence of truth
Hiding with wee clenched up toes
In Grandpa's scuffed-up tennis shoes
Far too large with experience
For such a treasured innocence
The untried ways of pure youth
Meet the untied ways of Grandpa's truth
The past and future mingle here
And grace the present with youthful cheer
What sharp rocks along the path
Have scuffed this Grandpa's shoes like that?
What travels could have scarred this leather?
Was joy or strife in each endeavor?
What path awaits these tiny feet
That race along and try to meet
The step of those who passed this way
Long before this play-filled day?
What obstacles will toughen hide
And bring on joy and tears and pride?
For someday soon, before too long
This child will put adult shoes on

And then the cycle will renew
And those shoes will be played in too
By another child with youthful dreams
Who too will love old shoes, and so it seems
Despite the paths we travel down
The path of life will circle round.

# Painting My Own Life

It is barely past dawn
The sun high enough
To give light enough
To see forever
A blank canvas before me
Glowing in its white nakedness
On tremulous feet, with shaking hands
I carry paint pots full of rich colors
And brushes, with wide soft tips
Toward the future
From nowhere, inexperience
Snares my childish foot
I stumble, paints splash
In a sparkling arch of color
Wonder shines thru them
They fall, splashing across the canvas
In a myriad of colors, patterns
Blending and running
Some in harmony
Some defy congruency
My brushes all lost in the high grass
I am undone
For years I attempt to finger paint
Corrections to the image
At times colors blend
In near perfection

Then a tad too much yellow –
Or red, or black, or blue, or green
And the picture falls into distortion
At last, I give up, beaten, spent
Believing my own lack of talent
On my knees
In defeat, with head bowed
Then the voice of truth
Whispers to me
I lift my head and gaze up
From this position
The picture before me
Is a masterpiece
Of Impressionistic art
My spirit restored
I hang the painting
In the center of my soul
I gather my brushes
From the tall grass
And once again
Take up the pursuit of
Decorating my life

# Artist And Art

A person taking
Odd bits of color
Odd bits of words
Odd bits of wood
Odd bits of metal
Odd bits of hair
Odd bits of anything
Into their hands
Irrelevant stuff
Unknown to itself
Yet once blended, meshed
Touched with hands of love
The kaleidoscope turns
The picture clears
The bits revealed as art
The person revealed as artist.

# The World Outside My Door

The world outside my door awakens
Shivering in the morning dew
The air cool and heavy from a night of rain
Morning fog, thick and grey
Fills the hollow
Scents of fall, damp leaves and earth
Lift to join the morning breeze
As the sun raises her orange head
Thin light tickles through thick foliage,
Just beginning to glow with autumn's palette
Shades of red and gold appear
Drizzled across the landscape
Pools of still rain water
Reflect the light in small patches
Strewn across the emerald blades of grass
Like small mirrors
Dropped randomly over night
By fairies in flight
Crows call plaintively for the sun to hurry
A hush falls, silently we watch
As she journeys upward
Over the colorfully frosted hill-side
Her warming rays dry the water
Droplets from everything they touch

Turning morning fog to mist,
Slowly swirling upwards
This day grows older
Until everything is caressed by the sun's gentle touch
A sweet smell of newly cut hay
Drying in the warm breeze floods the air
The autumn sky slowly slips off her grey morning frock
And dons her afternoon gown of deep blue
Decorated with billows of white cotton splotches
The suns golden light changes from muted to bright
The greens, reds and yellows frolic across the countryside
Nature twirls herself over the hills in a
dance choreographed by the Gods
While I sit and watch in wonder.

# Seed Plans

As the young seeds waited impatiently for the wind to pick them up for their long journey out into the world, they discussed their plans.

"I intend to set sail on a leaf in that creek over there by the meadow and explore far off lands."

"I'm going to land in that yard over there, attach myself to a dog's tail, climb off behind the couch, hide and watch TV."

"I want to float up in a tree, let a bird eat me and carry me far south where I will start a new family."

"I'm not going anywhere! I am staying right here! It's good enough for Mama and it's good enough for me."

"I'm going over that hilltop and see what's on the other side."

"I'm going to slip into a car and go for a ride to the city."

"I'm going to sail to the porch, grab hold of a pant leg, drop off behind the dryer and never be cold again."

"I'm going to float into the barnyard and make a cat sneeze!"

The other seeds looked at Timmy and shook their wings, he was always thinking of mischief.

Before any other little seeds could voice their plan the WHOOSH of the Wind's whistle sounded in the distance and the little seeds fell silent in anticipation, shivering as their ride drew near.

The gnat zig-zagging
Around my full coffee cup
Wants to drink, but drowns

# A Short Ride

We ride a giant gentle ball of blue
With shades of emerald green
In a vast, limitless space
Of which we know nothing

This earth upon which we all depend
Floats in an ocean of unknowable space
It forces us to recognize
The insignificance of the human race

We look around and we believe
That everything is real
But it's not, it's here today,
Yesterday's gone, tomorrow's surreal

And when this gentle giant orb
Has finally had enough
She'll shake her back and shed her tears
And our stay here will be up.

# Belief

When my life is nearing its fatal end
Will I think of all the things I've read?
Will all the ideas I've discarded as false
End up entwined in my thready pulse?
Will all that I've gathered and held so close
Turn out to be my own personal hoax?
Does the truth really lay out there somewhere?
A truth that never – not once – lived in here?
Will the words that I've written be discarded and burned?
And all of the time spent and hopes that I've yearned
Be gathered together as useless old trash
And silently dumped in the fire and be ash?
Probably so.
Real life exists in the folds
So pay attention.

# Dark Days Of The Soul

There seems a dark shroud hovering
The death of a good mood, not quite born
It tried to make its way here
But missed the rain – and
Stayed on the other side,
In the realm of nowhere

My mood is dark – the prognosis bleak
I've tried – I will try harder yet, but
I no longer have the energy to pretend
That anything except a miracle will save me now
It is the small insignificant cuts, slices and nicks
In a day that bleed my soul to death.

When a major vein is ripped
The emergency patrol appears from the left
Of my real self, and puts on tourniquets,
Adjusts meds, and places sweet smelling salve
On the most violated parts and the soul understands
That it is hurt, and it lays itself down to recover.

But these insistent, repetitive, small, gashes never
Trigger the alarm; they are just small seeping wounds
They merit no notice – it is assumed they will heal
Filled with mundane cobwebs to stop the loss

Of the inner life draining away
Time will scab and pucker the wounds into scars.

The loss of soul fluid goes on and on until – such as now –
The body is on the stretcher, and there is
No point in turning on the siren
Yet once more – from the cold, sterile, hard
Atmosphere of the morgue my soul awakens.

Throws off the death shroud, and staggers
To the hallway, shouting for help
The angels rush in, armed with soft cotton thoughts
And lavender compresses to ease a fever that was
Brought on by the effort of returning – to here
My question now is; can I do it again?
When I am so irrefutably tired
And – if I can't
And – my body lives to see tomorrow
Will it really be me?

# Personal Fear

The passing of time
The reality, frugality, finality of death
That there is no option to slow down and look things over
That any choice has more than a fair chance of being wrong
That no yesterday can be retrieved, tidied up, made correct
That each moment is already gone before it is ever noticed
That all actions – all actions – have consequences
And mistakes happen


The sun never fails
The one constant in chaos
Is that light returns

# Stay Or Go

Should I stay or should I go
This place is sad, yes this I know
But are there other places better
Or is it just the sunny weather?

That makes me wish I lived elsewhere
Instead of in this gloom and glare
I wish I had a crystal ball
Or a seer standing tall

To show me how to live this life
To make the most of all that's bright
Within the hours of each day
And help me all along the way

But no guidance is forthcoming
So I guess I'll keep on running
On this path that seems to head
Into tomorrow until I'm dead.

# Sadness

It settles in my eyes,
It infiltrates my brain
It makes my body heavy,
My heart can feel the strain.

I don't know where it came from
I don't know why it's here
I don't know what it wants with me
I only know the tears.

It slips into my consciousness
With the amber light of dawn
I never see it coming
It's just here, and then I'm gone.

It holds me in its evil grip
Till it finishes its task
Of making me a crazy bitch
While it hides behind my mask.

Then all at once it disappears
Like mist in morning sun
And leaves me used and wondering
What planet it came from.

# Ghosts In The Twilight

The reticent twilight
Fell in a rush
No warning, no lingering
Just a last whispered hush

I sit in the silence
While the fireflies come alive
And the ghosts of my past
Begin to dance round the fire

I watch in the alpenglow
As night fights the day
And wins that fierce battle
As the light drifts away

The dancers they spin
And they twirl about
They don't care if I cry
They don't care if I shout

They remain in the twilight
As night rapidly falls
I refuse to be bated
The hell with them all

I pick myself up
Knock the dust from my shoes
I'll not argue this point
I repeatedly lose

The past is the past
I cannot change a thing
And truth to be told
I regret not a thing

I head for the warm
Glowing windows of home
And decide to release them
ALL in this poem.

Danu falls as snow
Her essence solid in hand
Then melts at your touch

Winter as Diamond
Solid, shining, sharp edged, hard
Spring melts the diamond

# Looking Back

I sit in the warmth of the watery spring sun
I gaze all around me at the blessings I've won
I wonder out loud how did I end up with all this?
Then my eyes start to close and my mind starts to drift.

I see a frightened young girl lying alone on a bed
An infant child sleeping in a crib by her head
I can see she's been crying, she's ready to bolt
Afraid that all this requires more than she's got.

I reach out my hand, through space thick with time
I see her start up, as if her hand can feel mine.
"Don't be afraid, don't think that you'll fail
Your love for this child will steady your sail."

"You'll come through these waters, with colors flown high
Just hold on my girl, do what you know to be right."
As if hearing my voice she looked up through her tears
I believe she could see me through that space made of years.

She dabbed at her tears with the hem of the sheet
Then sat up and reached for the child fast asleep
She silently held him while he dreamed infant dreams
"I'll be here forever," she promised, "you'll see."

I open my eyes, but all I can see
Is the glittering sun coming down through the trees
I can't seem to make my body arise
Soon I am drifting and again close my eyes.

A young woman stands alone in a room
Her eyes, and her body reflect nothing but gloom
She is alone again, and this time makes twice
She's offered her heart for such a small price.

And it was accepted, but like all things held cheap
As time drifted on, she was easy to leave
In the room down the hall, I hear her son playing
He hasn't a clue what his mother's heart's saying.

She's hurt and she's frightened, sure that she's done
She just can't keep racing on this track that she's on
She's sure that it's best if she just goes away
She can't seem to make the decision to pray.

Again I reach out and scream with my heart
"What's the matter with you? Just look what you've got
A cozy warm house, there's a car in the drive
A job where they love you, but that's not the prize.

Stop girl and listen to that sound down the hall
That's the sound of your son playing Atari Fuse Ball
What else do you need when you have him right here
Let the rest of them go, they aren't worth your tears."

She cocks her head sideways, I think that she's heard
Then she shakes herself off, like a ruffling bird
She walks down the hallway to her son's bedroom door
He's in there playing on the carpeted floor.

She musses his hair, smells the scent of his skin
And knows that they're fine for the mess that they're in
"How about McDonalds?", she asks with a smile
"Just the two of us haven't been out in a while."

He grins at her quickly, then looks back at his game
"Sure Mom, that's great. Wherever you say."
She tells him, "Get ready." Then adds with a frown
"We might see a movie while we're out on the town."

I startle upright, but the warmth in the chair
Entices my body to settle back there
Again my eyes close and my mind drifts away
To another long past, and difficult day.

This woman's down, she's out for the count
No love can help her, not any amount
Now she's alone, no child here to live for
Her family all gone, her heart rent to the core.

But despite all the hopelessness there in her eyes
I recognize the spark and reach back through time
"Don't give up yet, ride your anger up high."
She looks up at the stars and screams at the night.

"If you really exist, if you really are there
Then now is the time to show that you care!"
And from a great distance of time and of space
I see the blessing of future fold her in its embrace.

The light hits my eyes, the sun's overhead
And I smile at the wonderful life that I've led
I head for the house, my heart full of love
For the blessings I've had, were all sent from above.

# My Life A Word

I am only one word in a simple poem
A poem about life, family, friends and home
An ode to the mysterious passing of time
One without meter, pattern or rhyme

Yet here I am snuggled in this stanza of life
I've spent time as mother, as friend and as wife
Yet this poem's final verse is yet to appear
And probably won't for many more years

# Baby Boy Lost

You were an infinitesimal dot
Unknown and unnoticed by others
Yet the source of love, joy,
Longing, pride and plans
By some

Then you lost your place, letting go
You were swept into the stream of oblivion
Your absence went unnoticed by others
Yet mourned greatly, deeply, terribly
By some

Thoughts of you bring tears of loss
Pain, disappointment, grief and guilt
Unasked questions, never to be answered
Misery felt, yet left unspoken
By some

Who are these hot, salty, tears shed for
How can you hurt for someone you never met?
How can you miss what you never had?
These questions contained in an infinitesimal dot
Will never be answered
For some
The answers lost into oblivion.

# What Should I Write

They say that you must write everyday
But what is it possible for me to say?
Do I write about who, or why, or when
What do I know about any of them?

Do I tell my most unsettling fears
Of things that may or may not appear
Of the many mistakes that I have made
Or the things that continue to keep me afraid?

Do I write about the red-tailed hawk that glides
Effortlessly against tie-dyed skies
A rust colored orb aloft on wings
Watching the earth for moving things?

Do I write about my insufferable rage
At this country's seeming inability to say
Maybe we don't know every earthly fact
Let us be quiet and listen with tact?

Do I write about the crunch of fall grass
As I travel the fields watching summertime pass
Or as I walk the berm of a county lane
The hot Indian summer begging for rain?

Do I write about writing and not wanting to
Yet having no choice in this thing that I do
Of trying to quit and utterly failing
As I sit at my desk with my aching heart railing?

As the need to write overpowers my brain
And my thoughts jump aboard a runaway train
I put pen to paper, write of life, love and hate
To question is useless, this is my fate.

# I Turned Forty-Eight

I don't care that my underwear is torn and ragged
Or that my hands are rough and my nails jagged
I don't care that my gray roots are showing
Or that the dust balls in the house are rapidly growing

I don't care that there's hair in my shower drain
Or that the weekend weather map shows rain
I don't care that my toothpaste tube is open and oozing
Or that it's my mind, not my weight that I seem to be losing

I don't care that the shoes under the table don't match
Or that my cupboard holds no emergency food stash
I don't care that I don't even know whose shoes they are
Or that I don't have enough gas to get very far

I don't care that the water bill seems to be lost
Or that their check was accidentally tossed
I don't care that the furniture grows dog hair
Or that my watch has disappeared somewhere

I don't care that on some days I act out and I'm rude
Or that my wrinkles are showing and I eat too much food
I don't care that my flower garden needs a good weeding
Or that all of my clothes have recently stopped fitting

I don't care that the rocking chair cushions are stained
Or that the porch floor is scuffed and needs to be painted
I don't care that the screen in the door is torn loose
Or that nothing I have seems to be any use

I don't care that my shower faucet has calcified
Or that there's a smell in the laundry room I can't identify
I don't care that the hair on my legs is too long
Or that the lyrics I remember seem to always be wrong


I don't care that there are major holes in my socks
Or that the Christmas list I started seems to be lost
I don't care that a new hole has appeared in the couch
Or that I forgot what it was I used to care about

I don't care that my window sills are full of dead bugs
Or that my favorite jeans now refuse to zip up
I don't care that I can't find the things I look for
Or that unexplained dirt shows up on my floor

I don't care that some, no, most people don't like me
Or that when strangers look, they don't like what they see
Cause I'm forty eight damn it! And that's good enough
To not give a hoot about any of this stuff!

# Glass

The only thing
Separating me from
The ocean
The rain
The seashells
Is this thin pane of glass
So fragile
Yet so impenetrable
I sit here
Safe and warm
While my soul yearns
To wade the ocean
To touch the rain
To gather sea shells
To shiver

# Fear

There are lots of fears we carry around
Like bugs and slugs and swampy ground

Of growling dogs and hissing cats
Of snakes and spiders and cornered rats

But the most common fear around today
Is the common fear of what will people say?

I like to pretend that I don't care
What people say when I'm not there

But the truth of the matter is clear to see
I care about what some people think of me

This sad little fact makes me act untrue
To a the most important person who

Deserves my utmost honesty
The person I lie to most is me

In this truth I'm not alone
This common fear's in every home

What color should we paint the house?
It must fit in, must not stick out

I'd like to wear this funky hat
But it's best I not go out like that

Be quiet now, there will be no yelling!
You know the neighbors will start telling!

We have to mow the lawn today
For heaven's sake what will people say?

So on we go, the decisions we make
Are all made for other people's sake

And so until we lose this fear
There will be no honest living here

So make a rule every day
To have no fear of what people say.

# Ghosts

The ghosts that live inside my head
Too much alive, not near enough dead
Haunt my days, by night they're gone
My sleeps never broken, but my days are long

They bring me sounds and smells and thoughts
They tell me much, they're over-wrought
The truth they seek, is from long ago
But how will it help for them to know?

They lead my thoughts down different paths
I feel their love, their fear, their wrath
But how to help them find their peace
To loose these bonds, their souls release

This question I sit and ponder long
Which way is right, which way is wrong
If questions are asked and answers received
Will this bring solace, their pain relieved?

Or will it only fuel the fire
Make things worse, reveal a liar
They say that truth will set you free
If this be so, then truth I seek.

# Hearing Is Simple

Hearing is the essence of simplicity
No muscles engage
No intent is necessary
You are – so you hear
You do nothing, yet sound takes place
Your mind wanders
Its participation unnecessary
Your mind noticing sound is listening
Hearing is simplicity
Listening is not

I close my eyes
I am still, I barely breathe
I bask in the sensations of sound without meaning
I do nothing, yet sounds occur
They enter my ears on their own energy
Without warning
Without my intent
I notice what I hear
Despite myself I notice
Hearing becomes listening
I am drawn in, I am active
The judge enters and takes a seat

Paying attention, forming unrequested opinions
Listening is much harder than simply hearing
I want to go back to the simplicity of hearing
Away from this intensity of listening
In time, with practice, listening may become easier
But listening will never become simple.

# Create Your Soul

Glimpse into the glittering light
Enchant a wind with celebration
Experience a night storm by yourself
Catch secret sacred rain in a forbidden land
Whisper your desire to the wild Gods of the forest
Create a sacred bond with the moon
Release imagination amid transformation

# I Am Tired

I AM TIRED of rushing, hurrying, pressing on, missing out, forgetting, remembering, forgetting to remember, remembering that I forgot.

I AM TIRED of walking, running, exercising, traveling the crusty edge, missing the gooey center.

I AM TIRED of attempting, wanting, wishing, trying, failing, failing to try, missing the point, pointing at what I'm missing.

I AM TIRED of staying, moving, needing, hoping, needing to move, but staying; needing to stay, but moving.

I AM TIRED of opposites that are the same, digging so deep that it turns shallow, scraping the surface then falling in too deep.

I AM TIRED of thinking, meditating, writing, thinking about meditating, meditating about writing, writing about thinking.

I AM TIRED of me, you, them, us, her, him, it, they, me that could be you, us that becomes them, everything that becomes nothing; and when nothing becomes everything, then I AM TIRED.

# Teddy Bear Angels

The little brown teddy
That sits by my bed
Is one of three bears
Or so it's been said.

There's one at Aunt Ruth's,
One at Freda's house too
The story that follows
I'm told is quite true.

In each of the homes
Where the bears went to stay
Was a gremlin of sorts
Who played tricks every day.

These Gremlins would hide
And move things all around,
You could never quite catch them,
There was never a sound.

But each one of us had one
This much was quite clear,
Cause things got misplaced
And sometimes disappeared!

So the bears came to stay
To guard our abodes,
To watch out for gremlins
Or fairies or toads!

Now these houses are blessed
By each bears tiny face
The bears work their magic
Keeping things in their place.

So if in the future
On some far away day,
You find you have gremlins
That have moved in to stay.

You must find a teddy
To sit in your hutch
To guard and protect you
Against gremlins and such.

Someday in the future
When I've passed away
And this teddy is homeless
Needing a place he can stay.

Remember these words
For their wisdom is true
**Teddies are better than riches**
And I give this one to you.

# Seed

Holding the future of itself within its dry husk
Varying shapes, sizes and colors
Scattered throughout this earth
Some randomly, some intentionally
A pod of future held within a glamorless shell,
All within it, presumably understood
Like grains of ocean sand,
Too common, too numerous to be considered.

Yet to think of the future held within a seed;
Where it might land,
Whose life it might touch,
What it may or may not bring,
May or may not effect,
May or may not cause,
Then what is held within a seed
Becomes fathomless magic.

# Meandered

I like the word meandered
It sounds like me and dirt
Me and dirt, walking sole to sole
Me and dirt, sitting cheek to cheek
Me and dirt
Me and earth
Choosing a path of our own design
Do not lead
For I shall not follow
Do not follow
For I may become lost
This meandered path of life
Is mine to travel
Alone – just me and dirt
In my own meandering way

# Letting Go

The simplicity of letting go
Muscles relax, emotions ease
You decide it is the end of the struggle
So it is
Your hold loosens, your intent softens
Letting go is temporarily giving up
Release is permanently letting go
Letting go is simplicity
Release is not

I let it, or him, or her, or them, or then – go
But within moments I snatch it back,
Holding it tighter, tighter still
After a time, I let it go again
Watching as it drifts a little further away
Panic strikes!
I retrieve it and hold it even closer
As easy as it is to let go, it is too hard to release
Like a cat with its prey
I let it go
Only to drag it back
But practice, practice, practice – catch and let go
The letting go times grow longer
The holding times grow shorter
I become bored with my prey
The life of it dwindles

And a day, or week, or month, or year
Or maybe a lifetime later
I realize that I have let it go to the point of release
And it is gone, forever
The simple repetition of letting go has brought about release
But release is never simple.

# Man Fails

We believe more luck makes another breeze
Almost happy between nature and machine
Man can't imagine life without green
But man fails to see what needs to be seen

# The Old Rusted Gate

The old rusted gate sits all alone
It leans against an old weathered post
Its days of necessity are long past
Its broken top hinge lost in tall grass

For many years I've passed this gate
I never noticed when it met this fate
But now it snags my full attention
I find I must not fail to mention

How time marches on if we're aware or not
How things important today are soon forgot
That the only constant is the constant change
That the world you see is limited in range


The time we spend in constant worry
Is almost as bad as time spent in a hurry
You cannot save time, it will not stay put
It leaves you without a backward look

So pay attention to your days
Don't hurry your precious time away
Cause time won't wait, and when it's gone
You realize that you didn't have long.

# Guidance To The New Manager

There is this crazy woman
Who hides and lies in wait
She greets me every morning
And sometimes she stays all day

I've never really met her
So I cannot tell her name
She's never drawn a paycheck
But she stays here just the same

Most days she's rather quiet
And goes about unheard
But when she starts her antics
The day gets quite absurd

I will have the file I'm needing
It will be right in my hand
Then all at once it's missing
Look Out! Strike up the band

The doorbell begins to clatter
The phone begins to ring
And everything that's asked for
Has simply gone missing

Then I'll hear her crazy cackle
She's just slipped out of sight
She's sure she's won the battle
And now we'll have to fight

I chase her round the piles of files
And up and down the stairs
Just when I think "I've got her now!"

She up and disappears

Some days she gets too tired to play
And the game comes to an end
The missing files turn up at last
And the letter I will send

So I leave you with this notice
So you can go about with cheer
It's not you that has gone crazy
It's that OLD WOMAN who lives here.

# My Life In Haiku

The rain is falling
My life is becoming full
Like a rain barrel

Drop by drop it fills
Till it runs over the side
Dripping down to earth

Bursting with more life
Than I can fully enjoy
The edges ragged

Words become more real
Than life's experiences
Life, more head, than heart

The tide must reverse
My soul must drink its measure
Life is lived, not thought.

# A Massachusetts Morning

Sea gulls take wing into the first rays of dawn
Gliding, soaring, spinning
Through the early morning mist
Above water alight with silver essence
In silence

I sit within myself and watch
Waves churn white froth
Against jagged, black rocks
Dancing in the crevices, before racing away
To hide

While my soul waits, quiet yet eager,
To glide thru the mist of morning,
To soar across waves' water spray,
To slam against the world in passionate embrace
To dance

# Rain Blessings

Blue and gray pouches crowd the sky, each filled to overflowing with sparkling diamonds that drop to the parched earth below.
**Blessings from God**

Tiny orbs that tinkle against the window pane, and glitter in the pale light as they stream toward earth to form puddles of all sizes.
**Blessings from God**

Small mud filled rivulets trickling to creeks that wind to streams that rush to rivers that race on to the oceans, taking all in its path.
**Blessing from God**

Harsh pounding droplets, beating and destroying, pushed with unmatchable force against everything in its path, washing all away.
**Blessings from God**

Some danced for, some prayed against, yet all are,
**Blessings from God.**

# Time's Progression

Oh let this summer light
That dances round this day
Stop the progress of man and time
And keep the winter dark at bay

Summers music quiets down
And the light begins to dim
Time progresses past its prime
And dark at last descends

There is music in the tree tops
As the light fades in the east
The darkness edges out the day
And time's progression leads

# Just Who'da Thunk It?

I drive along the black ribbon of highway
The red gloss paint shines in the oncoming head lights
The 200 horses strain forward under the hood
The brightly lit dash keeps me company
The road so familiar, I needn't stay.

My mind drifts back to the old rusted dodge
I called it green, but I had a choice of three
A two year old plays contentedly in the back seat
I stand patiently next to his window, eyes watchful
The hood up, waiting for someone to notice, I need a jump.

Who'da thunk it?

I turn into the long graveled driveway
That splits the yard, wedged between the woods
Deer, raccoons and possums watch me from the shadows
Of the trees and brush that grow along the edge
And spread for acres and acres beyond my sight.

I see my first apartment, in the bad part of town
The one foot strip of grass that was our yard
Between the porch and the sidewalk
My toddling son picks a dandelion and blows
He is charmed with its white fuzzy head.

Who'da thunk it?

I turn on the light as I make my way down the hall
The carpet deep and plush beneath my feet
The wall gleams with new paint
Pictures of generations watch my progress
In more ways than one.

That first apartment, just three rooms and bath
The path to the kitchen thru my bedroom
My window, two feet away from the drug dealer's window
The old woman upstairs, the older one downstairs
The roaches under the sink.

Who'da thunk it?

I walk into the bedroom lay down on my bed
It's huge to my way of thinking
Queen mattress, too thick for my old sheets
Thick piled comforter hugs my body with warmth
I look out my window and into the woods.

The house is old and cold and dark
There are blankets hung up like doors to conserve heat
My son's crib stands as close to the gas stove as safety will allow
My blanket and pillow wedged between the rolling legs under the
crib
For warmth's sake, for his sake, I'm close enough, if I'm needed.

Who'da thunk it?

I rouse myself and continue on, into my private bath
All the gleaming chrome and porcelain reflect my face

The bottles of varied substances for my personal perfection are scattered
Along the counter that extends from wall to wall
For a moment I have to think about where to start.

I wait for my son to fall asleep safely in his crib
I head for my grandmother's house, next door
A 5 gallon bucket in my hand, I need water to flush
She waits in her nightgown for my nightly arrival
I try to be quiet, even though we are both awake.

Who'da thunk it?

I glance at the picture of my son, next to my bed
Very tall, dark haired, good-looking man, with a goatee
Holding a baby, standing next to his petite blonde wife
They are all smiling, they are all happy, even the baby
I am happy – if only for that picture – it was all worth it.

I stand in the checkout line at Kroger's
Beside my slight, blonde-haired, green eyed, son
He looks up at me, and with worry in his eyes
His voice, croaking with change, and asks,
"Mom will I ever be as tall as you?"
How do you say, I doubt it? You don't
I say, of course you will, I have no doubt.

Who'da thunk it?

I look at the person in the mirror in my bathroom
I see crow's feet, tired eyes, pinched mouth,
Rounded shoulders, dimpled legs, fluffy tummy
Gray hair, ragged nails, hairy armpits
I see the results of hard work, determination and misplaced curiosity.

Yesterday, this person was a girl of possibility
Thin, strong, taught, fresh faced, bright-eyed
Tanned, smooth, confident, energetic, determined
Quick of tongue and foot, she believed in magic
But best of all, she was courageous.

Who'da thunk it?

# I Want

Do you believe that preemptive war is ever justified?
Do you believe that violence stops violence?
Do you believe that patriotism is akin to religion?
Do you believe that being a good patriot requires a leap of faith?
Do you believe that we should simply believe what we're told and never question the teller?
Do you believe that an eighteen year old dying alone, afraid, and in pain, on foreign soil, is better than dying before he was ever born?

Do you believe poisoning our air and water is worth the money?
Do you believe destroying forests will not destroy us?
Do you believe killing off various animal species will not affect human life?
Do you hear the voices of your children's children crying out for your help?

Do you believe that income is worth more than health?
Do you believe pieces of paper colored with green ink have any true value?
Do you believe that other societies and civilizations, whose ancient histories predate ours by thousands of years, should listen to us and do as we say?
Do you believe we have nothing to learn from them?

Do you believe that an embryo dying in a cold, sterile trash can, or being frozen into infinity, is better than sacrificing it for the health of future generations?
Do you believe in war, but not abortion?
Do you believe that turning the other cheek is everyone's responsibility, except yours?
Do you believe that we should hold those of different ethnicity outside our borders and yet have no outrage for the plight of the Native American Indian?

Do you believe in using fear as a weapon for control?
Do you feel anger and contempt for those who believe differently than you?
Do you believe that those who disagree with you should be silent?
Do you believe none of this is about you?
Do you get angry when I ask these questions?

I want to take the hand of one of you who believes these things, and ask, why?
I want you to tell to me. I promise to listen.
I want you to listen. I promise to explain.
I want each of us to hear the other.
I want us to come to a deep understanding that melts into agreement.
I want us to walk down the path of reason, mutual listening and shared conversation.
I want us to arrive at the place where tomorrow looks better than today.
I want us to arrive at a today that is an improvement over yesterday.
I want yesterday to be a lesson we agree not to forget.
I want to understand you.
I want you to understand me.

When we reach that place

I want to take your hand.
I want you to take her hand.
I want her to take another's hand, and on, and on.
I want our linked hands to crisscross back and forth across this country.
I want us to cover this land in mutual understanding, mutual respect and mutual truth.

Then a new day, a new world, a new life based on truth and reason will descend onto these lands, and a new America will be born. On that day we will state with truth and pride, WE ARE the UNITED STATES OF AMERICA."

That is WHAT I WANT.

# To Carolyn

Ella arrived on a sea breeze
Unexpected and unknown
She introduced herself with a whisper
On the soft edge of a gentle wave
As it lapped around my ankles

"This one," she said, "I want this one…"
Startled, I said "what one and who are you?"
"This shell, this blue one right here and
I am Ella."

Without further introduction, I knew her
Knew her as if she had been with me for years
She likes blue shells
Red ones will do
Or, if she has to, she'll take pink
She likes waves and sun and laughing
She has dark hair and brown eyes, with yellow sparkles
Like a cat, she tells me…

She dances and twirls in the ethos
Until her time arrives
She will lead, she will not follow.
You may go with her, or she will go alone.
She has no fear, only laughter. She is here to be in joy…

# Meandering Thoughts

The gorgeous days of honey sun and wind
Have run bare
Shadows soar through the storm
Chanting a sweet delirious symphony
Of our death
But I fiddle in the last light
Praying there is still time to play.

The Goddess of light is gorgeous
After a rain
Like a diamond mist
Languid and smooth
She soars through the forest
Playing see me as fast as you can.

I go to a hot summer garden
Delirious beneath a cool rain
With bare feet
And eat life raw
And see beauty in death
But still bitter on my tongue

The summer is about over
And a sad mist sits low in the sky
Light wind sings through the silent forest
As I watch it lick the bitter sweet ache away

I can only imagine
The taste of light
Or a spring moon
But I know they must be sweet

Between dark and almost morning
Dreams fall into a gray giggling breeze
And grow a future flower garden

# Slice By Slice

Sometimes, when I'm coming back
From the magical castle
Carefully creeping down the steep hillside
I will catch a glimpse of my home
Just a small slice of the whole
It usually makes me smile and think… home
Yet there are times when that small slice
Looks completely foreign to me
As if I have truly dropped
Into another time and space
It will take me several seconds
To place in my mind
What part of my world
That vision belongs to
These are the times
I know the portal really works.

# Hadley

Hello my precious Hadley
We're so thrilled you're finally here
We've waited with anticipation
For the best part of a year

We've plotted, planned and knitted
And we've decorated too
We tried to think of everything
That we should do for you

But now you've finally joined us
And our joy can't be denied
We welcome you Miss Hadley
With love and gleeful pride

# Evan

Little boys are sent from the land of miracles;
A place where magic and wonder are common
They come to rescue us from ourselves
To drag us out into the sunshine and make us
Turn over rocks and wade barefoot in the creek
That runs through the strand of willow trees
They come to teach us to ask why and how
And to wonder about if and could.

Boys are sent to us to keep us from forgetting
Who we really are.

Welcome baby boy.
May the future hold long, hot summer days for you and
me to search under rocks, and wade creeks; and
Long winter evenings to tell wild scary stories
and hide under the covers and giggle about the
monsters we intend to slay when the sun rises.
But for now sleep peacefully in this blanket
knitted with love just for you, for soon we must
follow the trail of adventure and rediscover
Who we really are.

# Kenley

Welcome home Miss Kenley
We're so glad to finally meet
The precious little bundle
That we've waited for with glee
Now at last you're with us
We couldn't be more pleased
To hold you in our arms at last
And give your cheeks a squeeze

We've been making plans for you
With lots of schemes for fun
But just for now
Rest peacefully child
For much too soon you'll be grown

But before we let that happen
We will do our best to see
That you have lots of kisses and fun
From Papa Tim and me

# Daddy's Girl

Little girls take daddy's hearts
And softly split them wide apart
They crawl inside, and there they stay
Forever plus a single day

Your life today will have to change
From the life you had before she came
There's magic in your brand new world
Hidden in the words "she's daddy's girl"

# Mama's Girl

Little girls are mama's pearls
They come to change their mama's worlds
They bring them love and joy and laughter
And things are never the same thereafter

Your life will now revolve around
This precious love that you have found
Your world is blessed, oh, yes it's true
For above all others, she will love you

# No Compromise

Why is it women don't compromise?
Cause they've paid a high price
To just get by
They've seen the worst
And they've seen the best
Now they need past you to see the rest

Why is it women don't compromise?
Cause they've seen the truth
Written in your eyes
If they give in now, if they let you win
They can only blame themselves
For the mess they're in

This is why women don't compromise
Cause they've seen the truth
Written in your eyes

# Truth

Truth is in the mind of the beholder
Just as beauty is in their eye
I search around corners, under boulders
But the truth lays silent, not even a sigh

Sometimes I know, I've finally found it
Only to find the other side
And yet my heart keeps nudging me forward
Knowing that truth is the only real prize

So I journey on, thru books, movies and papers
Speeches, classes, experiences and thoughts
Knowing I'm close, yet missing the answer
Maybe today I'll find the truth---or not

# Not Today

I cannot get from here to there
No matter how I try
It feels as though my thoughts cascade
Then leave me with a sigh.

When I am busy doing things
That disallow the chance to write
My mind appears to free itself
And creativity takes flight.

Yet nothing will remain of those
Times of fruitful fancy
It all will disappear at once
Should I attempt to catch it

My memory will shift and spin
All within it lost
To some far-off forgotten land
Or in some ocean tossed.

Later, with my pen in hand
No thought that bears repeating
Will sift its way thru quickened sand
My mind again, retreating.

# Wine In The Afternoon

There's nothing quite like
Drinking wine in the afternoon
It brings on such illustrious ideas
Clears the mind
Makes understanding easy
It makes love not only possible
But necessary
Yes! Wine in the afternoon
Is the answer
To all of our problems